# Stories <small>IN THE</small> Clouds

## *Weather Science and Mythology*
## *from Around the World*

DOT TO DOT IN THE SKY

# Stories IN THE Clouds

## Weather Science and Mythology
## from Around the World

Joan Marie Galat     ILLUSTRATED BY Georgia Graham

whitecap

**LIBRARY AND ARCHIVES CANADA CATALOGUING IN PUBLICATION**

Galat, Joan Marie, 1963-, author
    Dot to dot in the sky : stories in the clouds / Joan Galat.
ISBN 978-1-77050-245-1 (softcover)

    1. Weather--Folklore--Juvenile literature.
2. Weather--Juvenile literature.  I. Title.

QC981.3.G34 2017          j551.6
C2017-905502-X

EDITOR  Patrick Geraghty
DESIGN  Andrew Bagatella

The publisher acknowledges the financial support of the Canada Council for the Arts and the Government of Canada through the Canada Book Fund (CBF). Whitecap Books also acknowledges the financial support of the Province of British Columbia through the Book Publishing Tax Credit.

Nous reconnaissons l'appui financier du gouvernement du Canada et la province de la Colombie-Britannique par le Book Publishing Tax Credit.

Canada Council    Conseil des arts
for the Arts      du Canada

17 18 19 20 21 22   6 5 4 3 2 1

Printed in Canada by Copywell.

OTHER BOOKS IN THE DOT TO DOT IN THE SKY SERIES:
- Dot to Dot in the Sky: Stories in the Stars
- Dot to Dot in the Sky: Stories of the Planets
- Dot to Dot in the Sky: Stories of the Moon
- Dot to Dot in the Sky: Stories of the Zodiac
- Dot to Dot in the Sky: Stories of the Aurora

OTHER TITLES BY JOAN MARIE GALAT:
- Dark Matters: Nature's Reaction to Light Pollution (Red Deer Press)
- Day Trips from Edmonton (Whitecap Books)

For Matthew, in all kinds of weather,
and for those who notice nature's more
subtle changes through the seasons.

# Contents

I love snow, and all the forms

    Of the radiant frost;

I love waves, and winds, and storms—

    Everything almost

Which is Nature's, and may be

Untainted by man's misery.


*Percy Bysshe Shelley*

# What Will the Weather Be?

**S IT GOING** to be sunny tomorrow? Will it ever stop raining? When will it snow? We ask these types of questions because the weather impacts us every day. The weather affects how we dress for the day. It affects whether we walk, drive, or take a bus. It affects our plans for outdoor activities, especially if we need wind for flying a kite, calm weather for playing tennis, rain for the garden, snow for skiing, or ice for skating. We want to know what the weather will be like before we plan a picnic, ball game, or bicycle ride.

The weather even impacts what kinds of houses are built in different climates. People living in areas with a lot of snowfall need steep roofs so that the snow will slide down to the ground. Those in hot areas may use awnings to shade their windows. Folks living in places that receive a lot of rainfall must have houses on stilts, or eaves and gutters to direct rainwater away from the foundations of their homes.

Because weather has such a great influence on daily life, people have always watched the sky, noticed patterns, and tried to figure out what type of weather was coming. Early cultures tried to predict the weather based on observations of astronomy and the ways the weather changed throughout the seasons. Indigenous tribes even tried to change the weather with rain dances, charms, and prayers.

Since the earliest civilizations, people from all over the world have noticed that dark clouds bring severe storms, rainbows appear after rain, and seasons change in a regular pattern. They noticed these connections, but did not understand the scientific causes behind them. As a result, they made up stories to explain why wind, rain, thunder, lightning, clouds, fog, and other types of weather occur. They also tried to predict the weather and made up sayings to describe the types of weather they witnessed.

Today we know much more than ancient cultures knew about the weather, but we are still learning. The study of weather is a science called meteorology. Scientists who study weather patterns and ways to predict what types of weather will occur are called meteorologists. They use satellites to watch weather and computers to help predict what will happen next. These tools make it possible for scientists to warn people when weather conditions become dangerous.

Countries around the globe share information about the weather through a United Nations agency called the World Meteorological Organization (WMO). Weather crosses all borders, but sharing weather information allows meteorologists to make important predictions that can prevent property damage, as well as injury and loss of life.

## WEATHER AND CLIMATE

- Meteorologists analyze and describe weather based on the conditions of the air around the Earth at a particular time and place.

- Weather descriptions can refer either to the present, or to a specific time span in the near future. They include whether or not the air is dry, humid, or holding precipitation such as rain, sleet, hail, or snow. Weather includes air temperature (measured in degrees), air movement (such as wind), and whether or not clouds are present in the sky.

- Climate refers to the history of weather in an area. It describes the daily and seasonal patterns of weather that have occurred over a period of many years.

## LAYERS OF THE EARTH'S ATMOSPHERE

☼: All of the Earth's weather takes place in its atmosphere—the air held close to the Earth by gravity. The Earth's atmosphere is made up of layers, and most weather occurs in the troposphere—the closest layer to the Earth. The troposphere reaches 11 miles (17 kilometers) above sea level over the equator and about 5 miles (8 kilometers) above sea level over the poles. Very little weather occurs in the next layer, called the stratosphere.

☼: The ozone layer protects Earth from harmful radiation. Ninety percent of the ozone in our atmosphere lies in the stratosphere.

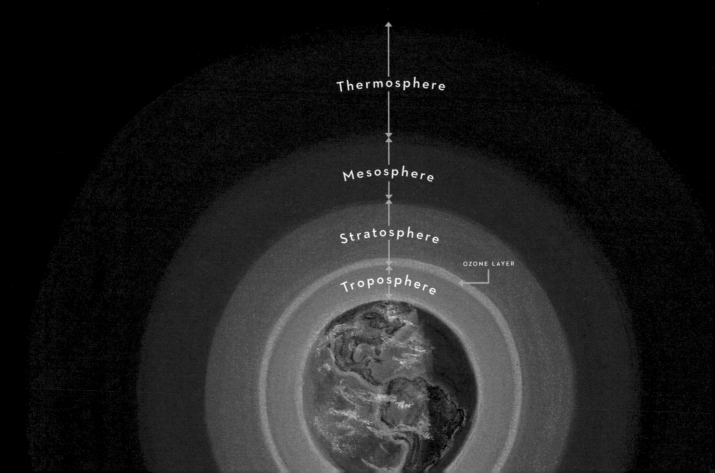

# Traditional Weather Forecasting

**SAYINGS AND PROVERBS** about the weather have developed over many centuries in all parts of the world. Scientists have examined different ideas and found that while some are more-or-less true, others can be misleading. For instance, "When clouds look like black smoke, a wise man will put on his cloak," is a true statement because clouds that contain large water droplets and ice crystals are darker. If you see a dark cloud coming your way, you had better cover up. On the other hand, the expression "Clear Moon, frost soon" would seem to be true, as the temperature may drop when you see the Moon shining in the sky, but this is not the whole story. Air is colder when there are no clouds in the sky to trap heat, so when the Moon shines brightest on a cold, cloudless night, frost may indeed soon appear . . . but this is also the case on any cold night, with or without clouds, even with no Moon at all.

Other sayings may be correct in one part of the world, but not in another, such as this one about the sunrise and sunset: "Red at night, sailor's delight. Red sky in morning, sailor's warning." The reddish color in sunrises and sunsets can indicate specific air conditions on the horizon, but this saying is more accurate in places where the weather moves from west to east, and less true in places where high-level winds change direction.

Another way people have tried to predict the weather is by observing animal behavior. You may have heard things like "When hornets build nests on treetops, a mild winter is ahead, while nests built closer to the ground mean a harsh winter is coming." It is important to realize that animals can only respond to changes in weather as they occur; they cannot react to changes that have not yet taken place. For example, people have noticed spiders spinning webs after a rain. This led to the saying, "When spiders' webs in air do fly, the spell will soon be very dry." If this forecast is sometimes reliable, it's not because spiders have a way of predicting weather. Instead, spiders build webs when it's dry because rainfall causes water droplets to stick to their webs, which makes them visible to prey. While the saying assumes it is a sign the weather will stay dry, rain may recur whether or not spiders choose to build webs after a rain shower. They take a chance at the start of dry weather, perhaps simply feeling quite hungry after a long rain!

Although animals cannot predict weather, observing their behaviors can sometimes provide clues about conditions that may arise. A science called biometeorology looks at the relationship between living things and the weather. Some animal species are sensitive to changes in the air pressure that occur as storms develop. An approaching storm might cause bees to return to their hives, frogs to call more, or birds and bats to change their migratory behavior by flying lower.

Some folks say you can figure out the temperature by counting cricket chirps. This method is called a "poor man's thermometer." To test it for yourself, count the number of times a cricket chirps in 14 seconds, then add 40 to get the temperature in degrees Fahrenheit (for Celsius, count the chirps for 25 seconds, divide that number by 3, then add 4). Even though crickets chirp more when it is warm, this method is not always a reliable way to estimate temperature as they are also noisier at night.

Some sayings aim to predict weather based on plant growth, such as this English proverb: "Onion's skin very thin, mild winter coming in; onion's skin thick and tough, coming winter cold and rough." Such phrases cannot be accurate since plants only respond to weather conditions as they occur, and any sayings that refer to weather in future seasons cannot be relied upon.

## GROUNDHOG DAY

Groundhog Day is recognized every year on February 2. According to legend, the groundhog sleeps all winter, finally coming out of his den on February 2. If he sees his shadow, he will become frightened and rush back inside. This is said to mean that winter will continue for six more weeks. If the groundhog does not see his shadow, spring is supposed to arrive soon. If you watch the news on television on Groundhog Day, you will see weather reporters at different zoos waiting for groundhogs to wake up. Of course this is all done in fun, since animals cannot actually predict the weather.

## PROVERBS ABOUT THE WEATHER

- Rings around the Moon, rain by noon. Ring around the Sun, rain before it's done.

- When March comes in like a lamb, it goes out like a lion.

- When sound travels far and wide, a stormy day will betide.

- When black snails on the road you see, then on the morrow rain will be.

- If the rooster goes crowing to bed, he'll certainly rise with a watery head.

# How Raven Brought the Sun

———— ☁ ————

{ T L I N G I T }

Long ago when the world was young, day was as dark as night. It was very hard to see, and people could not do many of the things they wanted to do. They did not know what their families looked like. They did not know when to wake up and when to sleep. They did not explore the world.

Because of this, people often sat in the dark and told each other stories to pass the time. One story was about a sky chief who lived high in the far-away mountains, and who was said to possess a large collection of treasures. Among these treasures was light itself, which the chief refused to share with the people of the world, even as they sat in never-ending darkness. The chief was also said to have a beautiful daughter, who he kept hidden away as if she were a treasure herself.

Raven heard the people tell this story over and over again, and decided to find out if it was true. He flew towards the mountains for a long time, never certain whether it was day or night. Finally he saw a faint light shining around a mountain peak. Raven tipped his wings toward the light, stopping only when forced to rest or to look for something to eat. When he was close to the mountain, he landed beside a stream to sip some water. Suddenly, Raven heard a sweet voice softly singing. He hopped along the shore towards the sound until he was close enough to spot a young maiden bathing in the water. She was the most beautiful person Raven had ever seen. He thought she must be the daughter of the sky chief he had heard so much about.

The maiden began scooping up water to drink from her hands. As he watched, Raven thought of a plan to find his way into the chief's home. He used his magic to turn himself into a speck of dust and dropped into the water just as the maiden lifted it to her lips. She drank the water with the speck of dust, finished bathing, and returned to her father's teepee on the mountain.

Raven's magic was powerful enough to turn himself from a speck of dust into a tiny baby. The maiden did not know why her stomach grew round until one night she woke up with a baby boy lying beside her. The maiden and her father loved the baby, who was really Raven. They admired how fast he grew and how quickly he learned to crawl and explore their home. Whenever he could, Raven crawled about and searched the teepee for the chief's treasure, but he could not find it. Finally he noticed three bags tied high up on the walls of the teepee. Each bag was tied shut with twine and glowed with an eerie brightness. The largest bag was the brightest and the smallest bag was the dimmest. Raven knew the bags must contain the treasures of light.

One day the daughter saw how deeply the baby slept and decided it was safe to leave him alone in the teepee. As soon as she was gone, Raven turned himself back into a bird and flew up to the bags. He tried to untie a bag, but the knots were too tight for his beak to get apart. He pecked at the twine, tugged at the ends, and tried to rip the sack open but he could not. He wondered if he could fly carrying the bundle, but heard voices outside the teepee before he could even try. Raven swooped to the floor and turned back into a baby just as the maiden and chief walked in.

Raven began to cry loudly. His mother ran and scooped him up but he did not stop howling. The chief offered him food, then water, but the child only cried harder.

"What do you want?" cried his mother.

Raven pointed to the bags.

"Please, father, let the boy play with a bag," said the maiden. The chief loved the boy and did not want to hear him cry. He reached up and untied the smallest bag. Raven stopped crying as the chief set the bag on the floor. He began to play with the bag by rolling it around the room. The chief and his daughter watched him carefully for some time but after a while they became bored and decided no harm would come to the treasure.

When Raven saw that they had stopped paying attention to him, he rolled the bag to the center of the room and tore it apart with his hands. The chief heard the bag rip and lunged toward it, but it was too late. Stars rose up in a stream of light and escaped from the teepee through the smoke hole. They scattered into the night, some forming beautiful dotted pictures in the sky. Far away, the people in the world noticed the twinkling lights. They were filled with delight but the chief was enraged. He did not want his precious treasure to belong to everyone.

Still, the chief knew he could not change what had happened and he loved his grandson very much. Unable to stay angry, he forgave the child for losing the treasure.

Raven spent his days crawling about and enjoying the attention everyone gave him. All the while, he was waiting patiently for another chance to trick the chief. It was several weeks before he found an opportunity. The chief and his family had stayed up late to celebrate a successful hunt. They had made themselves a great feast and passed the time singing songs and telling stories. The next day, everyone was very tired. They did not talk much and when they did, they often argued.

Raven began to cry. Once again his mother and the chief tried everything they could think of to console him. They offered him a bone with delicious meat clinging to it but he threw it to the floor. They offered him some cool water and he pushed it away. They tried to make him laugh with funny faces but he only cried more loudly and pointed at the bags hanging from the teepee. Finally the tired chief could no longer stand the noise. He reached up and tossed the child the second largest bag.

Raven immediately stopped crying. The chief watched him closely but relaxed when he saw the child was only playing and not tearing at the bag as he had done before. Raven rolled the bag across the floor, back and forth, slowly working his way towards the open flap of the teepee. When the chief glanced away, Raven rolled the bag outside and quickly tore it open. The chief and his daughter looked out to see what he was doing just as a bright shining object sailed out of the bag and up into the sky.

"The Moon is loose! Come back!" shouted the chief, but there was no way to make it come it back. The Moon nestled amongst the stars and has stayed in the night sky since that day.

The people of the world were very happy. Now they had enough light to see each other's faces and could walk without bumping into things. The chief was very angry for he realized he had made the same mistake twice. Nonetheless, the chief loved his grandson very much and forgave him once again.

"He is only a child and sometimes children do things they don't mean to do," he said to his daughter.

Raven was pleased with the light he had released into the world but more than ever he wondered what was in the last bag. He knew it would be much more difficult to trick the chief into giving up his largest treasure. Much time would have to pass.

Raven thought hard for several months. Then, one morning when everyone else was up, Raven opened his eyes but did not move from the spot where he had slept. His mother tried to coax him up but he would not move. She called the chief but he could not get him to rise either. Raven did not get up the entire day. When his mother offered him food and water he turned his head away.

"I don't know what to do," she said to the chief. "What if he is never well again?"

Raven heard her words and began to cry. He howled and shrieked as tears streamed down his cheeks.

"What can he want?" cried his mother in despair. Raven pointed at the last bag and began crying even harder. His mother pleaded with the chief to give the child the bag, but he folded his arms and refused.

"Would you let your own grandson die, rather than let him play with your treasure?" asked the chief's daughter. "Is that bag more important to you?"

The chief felt ashamed. He did not think a treasure was more important than his grandson's life. He reached down and gave Raven the bag. Raven stopped crying, but still did not get up. He let his mother feed him and the chief realized the child was too weak to let the treasure out of the bag. The chief stopped worrying and went outside.

The mother was tired from taking care of the sick child all day and lay down beside Raven. She thought she would rest for just a moment, but instead she fell into a deep sleep. Raven watched her chest rise and fall in even breaths and knew she was truly asleep. He turned himself into a bird and grabbed the bag in his claws. Raven lifted the bag up and flew through the teepee's smoke hole into the open air. The bag was heavy. He landed on the ground outside just as the chief spotted him.

"Raven is the one who's been stealing my treasures!" he shouted.

The chief ran towards the bird but it was too late. Raven had loosened the knot just enough for the Sun to float out and rise into the sky. Raven flew to safety as the chief shouted after him. The noise woke up the chief's daughter. She ran out of the teepee and stood in surprise as Raven flew away.

The people of the world were thankful for the Sun and the light it shone upon them each day. Now they knew when it was day and when it was night. They knew when to work and when to rest.

Raven was happy to be on his way home but was surprised when he arrived because nobody recognized him. The bird was covered in soot from squeezing his way out of the teepee's smoke hole and to this day all ravens are black.

Other Indigenous cultures, including the Inuit and Aleut, also tell of a large black bird, sometimes a crow. By bringing daylight to the north, it ends the long periods of winter darkness.

## THE SUN

- The closest star to Earth, the Sun is about 4.6 billion years old. The temperature of the Sun's disk—the part of the Sun we can see—is around 10,000°F (5,500°C).

- The Sun's energy, which causes uneven heating of our atmosphere, produces wind, clouds, precipitation, and every other type of weather on Earth.

- The Sun's size is described by its radius—the distance from its center to its surface. Its radius is approximately 432,000 miles (695,500 kilometers). The Sun could hold more than 1.3 million Earths, and 109 Earths would fit across its disk.

# Calabash of the Winds

☁

{ H A W A I I A N }

**M**AUI WAS A powerful Polynesian god, but when he was still a boy he sometimes found himself feeling restless, with nothing to do to pass the time. On one occasion, the day was not warm enough to make him feel like swimming, nor cool enough to make him feel like running races with his friends. Instead, Maui sat with his back against a palm tree, gazing at the clouds and daydreaming, until he happened to spot an osprey. He watched the osprey riding the breeze high above him, and it gave him the idea to build a kite.

Maui walked to the bamboo grove and cut enough wood to form a frame for his kite. Next, he gathered stems from the olona plant and weaved them together to make a strong twine. Maui's mother, Hina, saw what he was doing and gave him some of the tapa cloth she made out of tree bark. Hina was the goddess of the underworld and the patroness of arts and crafts. Her tapa was incredibly strong, as well as beautiful. Maui worked on his kite and his friends gathered around to watch him put it together. He worked for a long time and when he was done, his friends stared in awe. The kite was bigger than a palm tree.

Followed by his friends, Maui carried his kite to the beach. He laid it on the sand and began to unwind some of his twine, making sure to stay away from the trees near the shore. Although Maui was only a boy, he was a god with great powers, and he used his magic to make the kite fly. Despite the calm air, the beautiful kite sailed upward and danced before the sky.

It looked glorious! The twine gently tugged against Maui's hands as the kite bobbed in the air, and he began to wonder how well it would fly in a strong wind. Maui decided to visit the old priest who kept the winds in a set of gourds called calabashes, and his friends followed him to the priest's home—a place called the Cave of the Winds.

"Keeper-of-the-Winds," called Maui into the cave, "come see the kite I hold in my hands. Would you not like to see it fly with the power of your winds?"

The old priest came out into the sunlight and blinked at the mighty kite. "Surely, I would like to see that," said the Keeper-of-the-Winds, "but are you strong enough to hold the kite?"

"I am," said Maui. The Keeper looked at Maui sternly for a moment. He was not so sure Maui knew how strong his winds could blow. The Keeper opened a calabash called Ipu Iki but only let out his most gentle wind. The breeze was so weak it could not raise the mighty kite off the ground. It was only strong enough to rustle the tapa against the kite poles.

"We need more wind," said Maui. This time the Keeper opened the calabash wider and the wind that came out was stronger. Caught in the sudden breeze, the kite rose up into the sky. The tapa fluttered and flapped against the bamboo frame, forcing Maui to hold tight to the rope as it tugged against his arms. Maui braced himself against the earth. What a thrill it was to challenge his strength against a steady wind! His friends cheered and Maui was pleased at their admiration. The Keeper-of-the-Winds looked on.

After a short while, Maui felt sure the kite would not slip from his fingers and he wanted a greater challenge. "Please," he said to the Keeper-of-the-Winds, "release a more powerful wind."

The old priest hesitated. He alone knew the true strength of the winds in the calabash. He knew they could whirl and twirl out of control for very long periods of time. It was often quite difficult to get the winds back into the calabash.

"Come back another day," he said to Maui, hoping the boy would give up. Maui did not like being refused. He tried again: "Keeper-of-the-Winds, share your wind with us today. No harm will come to a god with my power and I can see you are enjoying the kite as well."

The old priest was having fun, so he gave in to Maui's charm and opened the calabash a bit more. This time the Misty Wind came out, followed by the Dusty Wind and the Smoky Wind.

Maui was thrilled as the kite flew first one way then the other, as the winds collided against each other in the sky. His friends cheered and wished they had kites too as they watched Maui's kite soaring high above them. The Keeper-of-the-Winds was delighted to see the pleasure on the boys' faces but his smile disappeared when Maui said, "See how easy it is for me! Now I must try an even stronger wind."

This time the old priest refused to give in. "That is enough for today," he insisted, closing the calabash. "The winds must rest and you must go."

Maui did not argue, for it had occurred to him that flying the kite would be even more fun if he had enough cord to sail it higher into the sky. He reeled in his kite and went home, but was already planning to return the next day. He spent the evening twisting more olona plant into twine.

Soon after the Sun rose, Maui carried the kite and extra twine to the Cave of the Winds. Once again, his friends followed him. "Keeper-of-the-Winds," called Maui, "I want to fly my kite today." The old priest came outside. He had spent the night thinking about Maui and his kite and he knew no argument would stop the young god from thinking he was more powerful than the greatest wind. Still, he tried again. "Maui," he said, "I can give you the mightiest of winds, but you will surely regret asking me to set them free. They have the strength to blow for many days. They will lift away huts and blow torrents of rain upon your people."

"I want to fly my kite," insisted Maui. "I am strong. They will not beat me."

The priest sighed and opened the calabash. Out tumbled the North Wind and the West Wind. Almost immediately the air cooled and the sky darkened as the winds pushed wisps of cloud together to form gigantic storm banks of the darkest gray color.

Maui was delighted and threw his kite into the air. He thrilled at the force he could feel rippling through the twine, as the wind whipped the kite across the sky. Suddenly the twine was nearly torn from his hands. It was tugging so hard, Maui began to fear the beautiful tapa cloth would be torn to shreds. He struggled to wrap the twine around both hands and braced his feet into the ground. His friends ran for cover, but Maui did not mind facing the storm without them. He loved the power of the wind.

The Keeper-of-the-Winds tried to put the lid on the calabash but the wind tore the lid from his hands. Now all four of the great winds were loose. The South Wind and the East Wind formed a howling gust so powerful that the twine broke away from the kite. Maui almost fell over as his kite sailed over the mountains and out of sight, the twine still whipping madly in the wind.

Maui helped the old priest put the lid on the calabash and left him alone to coax the winds back inside. Angry the wind had beaten him, Maui used his powers to turn from a boy to a giant. He grew so large, each stride took him across great stretches of rainforest. Stepping over the mountains in his search for the kite, he finally spotted its tattered and bent pieces lying on the ground near a stream. Maui bent down to pick up the broken poles and roll up the tapa. He carried the parts home, planning to use what was left to make a smaller kite.

Maui made himself the size of everyone else as he approached his home. When he arrived, no one answered his greeting or welcomed him home. Their huts were torn apart and their belongings were scattered. They blamed Maui for calling out the mighty winds.

After that, Maui flew his new kite without asking for help from the Keeper-of-the-Winds. He began to notice that his kite blew in one direction before the rains came and another direction when the weather stayed dry.

One day, he saw some people from his village going to collect poi and warned them the weather was about to turn wet. They would not listen to him and came home soaked from the rain. Another time, he heard some women talking about whether or not it was a good day to lay tapa out to dry. He told them it would be warm for several days.

People started to pay attention to Maui and forgave him for the trouble he had caused. Even the Keeper-of-the-Winds saw that Maui had learned he could not control the winds, and he came out of his cave once again to watch the boy fly his kite.

## WIND

☼ Winds are named according to the direction they come from. For example, a west wind comes from the west and a north wind comes from the north.

☼ It tends to be windier high above the ground because trees, buildings, and other objects cause friction that slows winds near the Earth's surface.

☼ Winds occur because different surfaces such as land and water absorb the Sun's heat unevenly, creating areas with different air pressures.

☼ Low-pressure areas form when air temperatures increase over a warm piece of land or ocean. The heat causes air molecules to move faster and push harder on their surroundings. The mass becomes larger as the particles create more space for themselves and the hot air becomes less dense than the cooler air around it.

☼ When air over a cold area of land or ocean cools, the air becomes more dense as air molecules move slower and the surrounding air pushing on them causes them to take up less space. As the air grows denser, it pushes warmer air upwards. The sinking air mass causes high air pressure.

☼ After warm air rises, it cools and sinks back down, pushing more warm air up. This process is called convection.

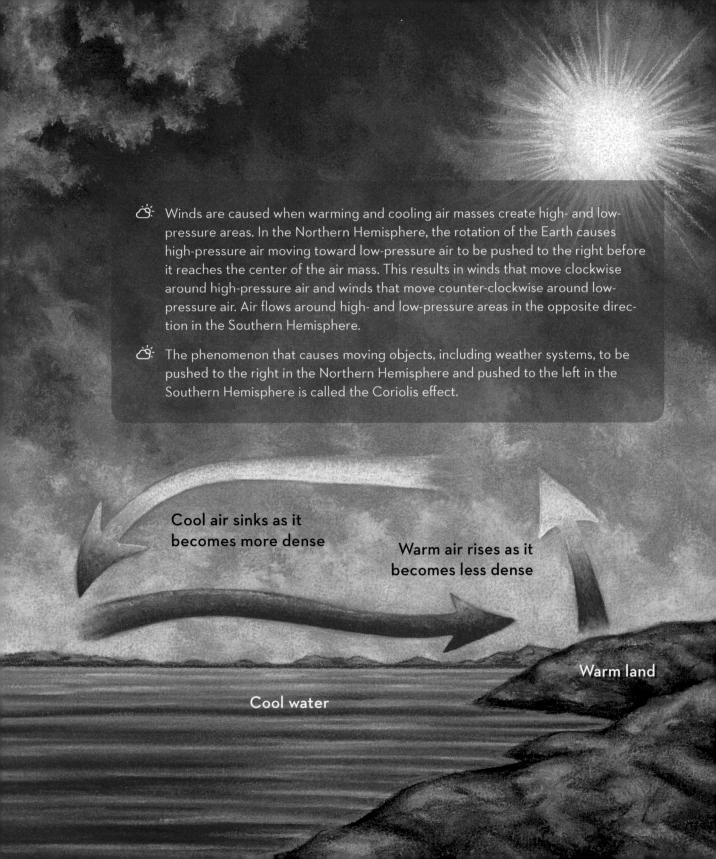

Winds are caused when warming and cooling air masses create high- and low-pressure areas. In the Northern Hemisphere, the rotation of the Earth causes high-pressure air moving toward low-pressure air to be pushed to the right before it reaches the center of the air mass. This results in winds that move clockwise around high-pressure air and winds that move counter-clockwise around low-pressure air. Air flows around high- and low-pressure areas in the opposite direction in the Southern Hemisphere.

The phenomenon that causes moving objects, including weather systems, to be pushed to the right in the Northern Hemisphere and pushed to the left in the Southern Hemisphere is called the Coriolis effect.

Cool air sinks as it becomes more dense

Warm air rises as it becomes less dense

Warm land

Cool water

## VIOLENT WIND STORMS

A tornado is a violent and destructive whirling wind. Its funnel-shaped cloud passes over land in a narrow path. Tornadoes have the highest winds on the Earth's surface, with speeds as high as 300 miles (480 kilometers) per hour.

A hurricane is a tropical storm with winds moving at a speed of at least 75 miles (120 kilometers) per hour. Winds near the storm's center may reach 200 miles (320 kilometers) per hour. This type of storm is called a hurricane in the North Atlantic Ocean, Caribbean Sea, Gulf of Mexico, and eastern North Pacific Ocean. It is called a typhoon in the western Pacific Ocean and a tropical cyclone in the Indian Ocean.

# The Thunder God

☁

## { CHINESE }

IN CHINA, THE god of thunder is called Lei-Gong. He bangs a hammer upon a drum to make the clouds roll and rumble into each other. Every time Lei-Gong strikes his drum, rain pours in torrents to the ground.

Long ago, there lived a peasant who would shake his fist at the sky and shout curses at the clouds every time the thunder began to rumble. He did not like rain, noise, or lightning, and especially did not like his crops being drowned. Lei-Gong was angry at the peasant's curses and temper. He always made sure his darkest clouds rained on the peasant's field.

One night, the peasant woke up to see his field was once again soaked more than any other plot of land. He decided to make sure it did not happen again and came up with a plan to capture Lei-Gong. The peasant waited for a sunny day when the god of thunder was out of sight, then heated some iron and hammered it into bars for a cage. He made hinges, a door, a roof, a floor, and most importantly, a lock and key. It took three days to make the cage and another day to make the lock and key. When everything was done, the peasant was pleased with his efforts. Sturdy and strong, the cage would certainly hold the god of thunder. He dragged the cage into his garden and covered the top of it with garden cuttings and brambles.

Now the peasant was anxious for a storm, but the thunder god stayed away for quite some time. Leaves fell onto the cage, making it even more difficult to see. Finally, late one afternoon, the peasant heard thunder in the distance. He shooed his two children inside and watched the storm move closer. Finally the clouds were overhead. The peasant grabbed his pitchfork, shook it toward the sky, and shouted, "Come down and show me how great your power is on the ground!"

The thunder god was enraged to hear the peasant's challenge. Banging his hammer against his drum, Lei-Gong roared down a wind current and crashed to a stop before the peasant. Wasting not a second, the peasant raised his iron pitchfork and forced Lei-Gong to step backwards. The god tumbled backwards into the cage and before he could catch his balance, the peasant slammed the door shut and locked it.

Stepping back from the cage, the peasant cheered. "I've got you now, you bag of wind and air! You can't make rain from the ground now, can you!" He jumped about with glee. The peasant's children heard him and ran out of the house to see what had happened.

The god of thunder shook the bars and rattled the lock, but the cage was too well made to be so easily broken.

The peasant turned to his son and daughter. "Tonight we'll eat thunder stew! I'm going to town to get some spices at the market. Stay away from the cage. Absolutely do not talk to him and most definitely do not give him any water." Before they could ask a single question, their father was on his way and soon out of sight.

The children could not help being curious. Imagine having the god of thunder in your very own yard! They crept into the garden and looked at Lei-Gong. He did not look so ferocious up close. In fact he looked sad. The thunder god eyed the children watching him. He sighed a mighty sigh and a tear trickled down his face. "Oh, children," he said, speaking in such a soft voice they had to step closer to hear him. "Won't you let me go? I don't belong in a cage."

The girl, whose name was Nu Wa, felt sorry for Lei-Gong. She thought her father was being too harsh but she was too frightened to disobey him. Nu Wa needed to think. She told her little brother to go back into the house.

The thunder god tried again. "You are trying to be a good girl by listening to your father. I understand, but surely you could give me a drop of water. It is so hot and I am suffering terribly."

Nu Wa did not see what harm there could be in giving the thunder god a bit of water to drink. It was very hot and surely her father would never know. Besides, she was feeling even more certain that her father's hatred was unreasonable. Why could they not just get along?

She ran to the well and brought back some water, but was afraid to step close enough to hand it to him. "Please," she said, "go to the back of the cage and I will set the water down for you."

The thunder god did as he was asked and stepped back from the bars, never taking his eyes off Nu Wa as she set down the water. When she had returned to her spot, a few paces from the cage, Lei-Gong came forward, drank the water, and shouted with glee, "I am Lei-Gong, god of thunder!" As his voice boomed out, his body grew like a billowing cloud and burst out of the cage. Nu Wa's brother ran out of the house and stood beside his sister as bits of iron flew across the yard. Nu Wa stared in surprise, too frightened to even run. Lei-Gong turned back and said, "You were right to save me." He pulled a tooth from his mouth and threw it on the ground in front of them. "Plant this and use the fruit it bears to save yourselves."

The cloud rose into the sky and torrents of rain began to pour down. "Go inside!" Nu Wa shouted to her brother. They ran into the house and watched the storm from a window.

The peasant was almost home when the storm began and immediately he knew that the thunder god had escaped. He was angry with the children, but had no time to punish them. The rain was not lessening and their house was flooding. The peasant began work on a boat made of iron, while the children planted the tooth, hoping something would grow that would please their father.

The rain fell overnight and continued to pour the next day. The children stepped outside and saw the tooth had sprouted into a vine. Upon the vine grew a splendid flower. Almost immediately, the flower formed into a gourd. The gourd grew and grew, while on the other side of the yard the peasant formed sheets of iron into a boat.

The rain continued and the ground became so soaked that the water had nowhere to run. The Earth was flooding. The peasant climbed into his boat and the children, remembering the thunder god had said the tooth would save them, cut the gourd from the vine and sliced it in half to make their own boat.

The two boats rose with the water, higher and higher until they reached the home of the gods. The peasant banged on the gates of heaven and demanded to be allowed inside, but seeing a human at the gates did not please Gong Gong, the spirit of the waters. He commanded the water to disappear.

It took only a second for the water to be gone. The peasant and the children in their boats hurtled down to Earth, where it was already dry. The iron boat crashed to the ground and shattered, killing the peasant. The soft gourd landed with a thump but did not break apart. The children stepped out of the gourd and looked around. They were the only two people left on Earth and did not know what to do.

Black clouds blew across the sky and rumbled. A voice boomed from the clouds: "Remember, you were right to save me. Use the fruit to save yourselves."

The children walked back to the gourd and looked inside. They saw seeds that they had not noticed before. They pulled out the seeds, planted them, and used the plants that grew to help them survive. They learned to take care of themselves and to trust that being kind would help them in the future as it had helped them in the past.

## THUNDER AND LIGHTNING

Scientists estimate that lightning strikes somewhere on Earth 40 to 50 times every second, totalling about four million strikes each day.

Most thunderstorms happen in the late afternoon. They occur when warm, humid air rises into cooler air. The humidity in the air condenses to form clouds, ice crystals, and rain. Thunderstorms drop heavy rain for about 30 to 60 minutes.

When you touch a metal object on a dry day and feel a shock, you experience a phenomenon similar to lightning. Shuffling your feet on a carpet causes your body to attract excess electrical charges, and if you touch metal, these extra charges help create a pathway that conducts an electric current between your body and the object. In clouds, lightning forms much like static electricity forms on Earth. The movement and collision of ice particles in a cloud creates electrical charges. Charges near the bottom of the cloud affect charges near the Earth, creating a situation where the air in-between can conduct an electric current. The result is a bolt of lightning.

CONTINUED . . .

☼ Lightning can occur inside a cloud, between two clouds, or between clouds and the ground.

☼ Thunder occurs because the air around a lightning flash rapidly heats up. The air quickly expands and then contracts as it cools. This air movement creates the sound waves we hear as thunder. You can hear thunder as far as 25 miles (40 kilometers) away.

☼ Lightning will hit anything in its path, but it is more likely to flow through good conductors, especially metal objects (such as bicycles or golf clubs).

☼ It is important to find shelter inside as soon as you see lightning because storms travel very quickly. You should stay away from windows, avoid landline telephones, get out of the bathtub, and keep away from metal appliances. Stop using any computer that is plugged into power or connected by a wire to the Internet.

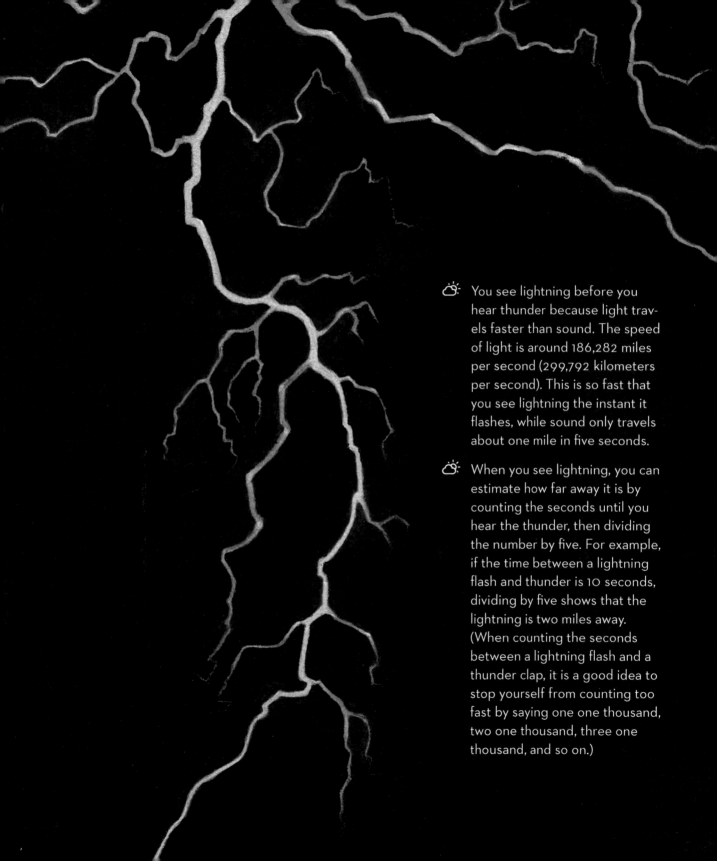

☼ You see lightning before you hear thunder because light travels faster than sound. The speed of light is around 186,282 miles per second (299,792 kilometers per second). This is so fast that you see lightning the instant it flashes, while sound only travels about one mile in five seconds.

☼ When you see lightning, you can estimate how far away it is by counting the seconds until you hear the thunder, then dividing the number by five. For example, if the time between a lightning flash and thunder is 10 seconds, dividing by five shows that the lightning is two miles away. (When counting the seconds between a lightning flash and a thunder clap, it is a good idea to stop yourself from counting too fast by saying one one thousand, two one thousand, three one thousand, and so on.)

# The Spider Weaver

### {JAPANESE}

A YOUNG FARMER named Yosaku worked the soil in his field to get it ready for planting. He worked slowly, for he was feeling sad. His mother had died a few weeks earlier and he missed her very much. It was hard to think of life without his dear mother.

As Yosaku leaned on his hoe to rest a moment, a sound near the ground made him straighten up and turn his head. He saw a snake slithering across the soil, moving towards the edge of the field and into a patch of wildflowers. Yosaku watched the snake wind its way up the stalk of a small bush and realized it was going after a spider that hung from a silken thread below its web. Without thinking, Yosaku raised his hoe and knocked the snake off the plant and away from the spider. The surprised snake wanted only to get away. It righted itself and slid off into the tall grass. Yosaku lowered his hoe. He did not want to kill the snake, he only wanted to stop it from harming the spider.

The spider climbed its thread to get a better look at the man who had saved its life. They looked at each other for a moment, then Yosaku returned to the field. He soon forgot about the spider and the snake as he spent his day working about the farm.

The next day, Yosaku was surprised to see a beautiful young maiden walking along the road towards his house. He quickly went inside to wash his hands and face, and when he came out, she was almost at the door. The woman bowed and spoke very softly. "I am a weaver, come to help weave your cotton into cloth. Would you like me to do this for you?"

"I would like that very much," said Yosaku, for he had not had new clothes for some time and was looking rather ragged. Yosaku led the young maiden to the room where he stored his cotton. She stepped inside and saw a chair, a loom, and great piles of cotton sitting in the sunlight that shone through an open window. She went to the loom and sat down, planning to begin as soon as Yosaku left.

"I will be in the fields if you need me," said Yosaku, and he stepped outside to continue his farm chores. By the time the Sun had nearly crossed the sky, Yosaku was finished his work for the day, and he went to see what the maiden had done. He thought she might have had trouble working a loom that was new to her and did not expect to see much cloth. However, when he stepped inside he saw that several bolts of fabric were neatly rolled into a pile. He counted them with amazement and said, "Surely you are the quickest weaver I have ever met. How did you get so much done in such a short time?"

She did not want to answer the young farmer's question, so she asked him a question back. "Are you happy with what I have done?"

"Indeed, I am," he replied. "But however did you work so fast?"

This time she tried to change the subject. "Tell me what you will do with the cloth."

"I will have new clothes," he said, "and sell what I do not need. But please, tell me how it is you have made fourteen bolts of cloth in just one day?"

Her answer made him even more curious. "You must not ask me questions about weaving and you must never watch me at work." Yosaku nodded and tried to respect her wish for privacy. Day after day she made more cloth, and day after day Yosaku wondered how she did it. But he did not ask her again.

One day, Yosaku's chores took him near the house. Only steps away from the weaving room window, the farmer thought, "What harm can there be if I watch her work? I mean her no harm." The farmer peered inside and his eyes opened wide at what he saw. The woman was nowhere in sight, but a giant spider stood in the room. All eight legs worked the loom, spinning the cotton it had eaten to make beautiful silken thread. Yosaku leaned closer to the window and looked hard at the spider. He recognized it was the one he had saved and realized weaving was the spider's gift of thanks.

At the end of the day, the maiden came out of the room, arms once again laden with beautiful, shimmering cloth. Before she went on her way, Yosaku thanked her politely as he did each day, for he knew she would be upset if he admitted he knew her secret.

This routine continued until Yosaku realized the maiden would soon run out of cotton. He rose early the next day to walk to the nearest village and buy some cotton at the market. Yosaku bought a very large amount of cotton, knowing it would not take the spider long to spin it into cloth, and on the way home he stopped to rest in the shade of some trees. He set the bundle on the ground and closed his eyes.

While Yosaku slept, the snake he had struck with his hoe made its way toward the trees. Recognizing the peasant, the snake became frightened and slithered into the cotton to hide. Yosaku awoke and picked up the bundle of cotton, not knowing he now carried the snake with him as well.

Yosaku returned home and knocked on the door of the weaving room. The maiden opened the door. "Thank you," she said. "I'm nearly out of cotton and this will help me make a larger piece of cloth." She closed the door, turned herself back into a spider, and began to eat cotton to make the thread. As she ate, the snake slithered out of the cotton and saw the giant spider. What a tremendous meal it would make! The snake flicked its tongue in and out, then lunged at the spider's nearest leg. Hearing the movement, the spider moved her leg just as the snake's jaws were about to snap. Startled, the spider climbed up the wall and out the window as the snake slithered after her. She could not move quickly after eating so much cotton, and the hungry snake was catching up. Just as the snake was about to lunge at the spider again, the Sun happened to look down and see what was happening. The Sun knew of the spider's kindness, for it had shone upon her and the cotton as she worked.

Reaching down to Earth, the Sun lifted the spider up into the sky. To thank the Sun, the spider used her gift of weaving to spin the cotton she had eaten into fluffy clouds. Thanks to the spider, the Sun could now enjoy privacy whenever it wanted by hiding behind the clouds.

This is why clouds look like large balls of cotton and why "kumo" is the Japanese word for both spider and cloud.

## CLOUDS

☼ When warm, moist air rises and cools, water vapor turns to water droplets and forms clouds.

☼ Cumulus clouds are the dense, fluffy looking clouds you see in different shapes, usually with rounded outlines and a flat base. They form when warm bodies of air rise. Large cumulus clouds sometimes become thunderstorms.

☼ Stratus clouds are large layers of clouds, sometimes hundreds of miles long and usually 2,000 to 7,000 feet (600 to 2,100 meters) high.

☼ Cirrus clouds are white, wispy, and very high up—20,000 to 40,000 feet (6,000 to 12,000 meters). They usually contain very small ice crystals.

☼ Nimbus clouds are rain clouds, and usually dark gray. When the word "nimbus" is added to the beginning or end of a cloud name, such as nimbostratus or cumulonimbus, you can tell the shape of the storm cloud. Cumulonimbus clouds are usually associated with hail, lightning, tornadoes, downpours, and flash flooding.

# How Glooscap Found Summer

{ M I ' K M A Q / W A B A N A K I }

LONG AGO, THERE was a place where it was always winter. The land was forever covered with snow and ice because the Ice King only allowed the Sun to shine for a short time each day. When the Sun disappeared each night, the wind blew the snow into hard and crusty drifts. The air was so cold, the people of the Wabanaki tribe could see their breath turn to frost when they stepped outside their wigwams.

The Wabanaki could not gather enough food in such cold weather. The plants they liked to eat were far beneath the deep snow, and the animals they liked to hunt often took shelter and could not be found. The people were weak with hunger and filled with despair. Master of all the Wabanaki, Glooscap felt bad seeing his people suffer from the never-ending cold. He decided to visit the Ice King and see if there was a way to make him go away and take the cold weather with him.

Glooscap began walking toward the Ice King's home in the far north. With each step, the wind became more bitter, the snow more crusty, and the air even colder. Finally Glooscap saw the Ice King in the distance. He was standing outside his wigwam, watching Glooscap approach.

The Ice King was very polite to Glooscap when he arrived. He welcomed his guest inside and offered him food, drink, and a comfortable place to sit and rest. Glooscap was tired from his journey and glad to sit down, but he did not forget why he had traveled so far.

"I am here because my people are tired of your cold winds, frost, and blowing snow," Glooscap told the Ice King. "You must move your home farther north."

The Ice King did not intend to move just because Glooscap thought he should, but he was clever and did not argue with his guest. Instead, the

Ice King began to tell Glooscap a story about one of his many adventures. Glooscap listened politely, unaware that the Ice King's helpers, Frost and Wind, were all the while weaving a spell around him. Soon Glooscap found it hard to pay attention to the Ice King's story. In fact, he wanted nothing more than to lay his head down and sleep. Glooscap closed his eyes, thinking, "I'll insist he move away after I rest for just a little while." He was so tired he did not even know he had stretched out on the floor of the wigwam. Glooscap slept and slept, and while he slumbered the Ice King made the world even colder.

Six months passed and the Wabanaki people wondered why their leader was not looking out for them. Finally Glooscap built up enough strength in his sleep to overpower the Ice King's magic. He woke up to see a loon waiting patiently at his side. It was Tatler, the tale-bearer. He had come to tell Glooscap a tale of a land far to the south where it was always warm and sunny. "Surely," said the loon, "the Queen of Summer will be able to overpower the Ice King." Glooscap thanked the loon and decided to go straight away to ask the queen for help. He knew he must hurry, for his people had been suffering such a long time.

Glooscap went to the sea and called for his friend the whale to rise and serve him. The whale surfaced and Glooscap leapt onto his back. "Take me to the South Land," he cried. "Travel at your quickest speed!"

"I will take you to the south," answered the whale, "but you must close your eyes and keep them closed while I swim. If you open your eyes, something dreadful will surely happen."

"My eyes are shut," said Glooscap. "Now swim!"

The whale thrust his tail against the water and they took off at a mighty speed. First one day passed, then another, then several more. The air became warmer with each passing day and the sweet scent of flowers wafted across the ocean. Glooscap could feel the Sun warming his face when he turned his closed eyelids toward the sky.

One day, the whale swam closer to shore than usual and the clams called out a warning. "Go back to the deep water, this is too shallow for a giant whale."

The whale did not understand the clams' language and asked Glooscap what they were saying. Glooscap did not know either, but he was so anxious to meet the Queen of Summer that he answered anyway. "They say hurry. You are close to the South Land. Go as fast as you can to get there!" At that moment, Glooscap broke the whale's rule and opened his eyes. He saw a land green and lush, and a sky the color of bluebells.

Suddenly the whale felt rough sand pushing beneath his belly. He became stuck in the shallow water and could move neither forward, nor back, nor side-to-side. Panicking, the whale tried desperately to free himself by thrashing his tail against the water.

Glooscap jumped off the whale's back and into the shallow water. He pushed against the whale's head until its massive body shifted away from the shore and back toward the deep water. "Thank you for bringing me to the land of summer," said Glooscap. He threw a pouch of tobacco and a pipe to the whale for a reward.

The whale was pleased with the gift and to this day is often seen in the distance with a plume rising from his spout as he smokes the pipe.

Glooscap turned away from the ocean and walked into a forest. He found a path and followed it to the highest point on the tallest hill. He could see a long way in each direction and spotted a wigwam so magnificent, he knew it could only belong to the Queen of Summer. Glooscap made his way toward the wigwam and when he finally arrived, the queen stepped outside, a garland of sweet-scented flowers forming a crown on her head. "I have come to ask your help in defeating the Ice King," said Glooscap. "My magic alone is not strong enough to save my people."

The queen replied, "I would like to help you, but I cannot leave my home for long or my own people will suffer. How will I find my way back again if I travel north with you?"

Glooscap took a knife and a moose hide and cut the hide into a long cord. "We will stretch this cord out behind us as we travel. You can follow it home."

"I will come for now and see what can be done," replied the queen.

Glooscap and the queen traveled through the land of summer, through forests and over plains to the North Land where Glooscap lived. As they traveled, the Queen of Summer warmed the air and the earth. The snow melted and the Sun shone, but the farther north they traveled, the more difficult it became for the Queen of Summer to use her magic. "The only way to beat the Ice King is face to face," said Glooscap. The Queen of Summer nodded her agreement, so they continued to travel north.

When they were almost at the Ice King's wigwam, the queen stopped and made herself invisible. The Ice King saw only Glooscap arrive and once again welcomed him inside his wigwam. He offered him food and drink and the most comfortable seat. This time, however, Glooscap did not accept the Ice King's offerings.

As they stood face to face, the Ice King noticed that puddles were forming inside the wigwam. The air was warm and his power could not overcome it. "What magic are you using?" he asked, becoming so warm that tears he had once cried as icicles rolled down his face.

The Ice King's tears made the Queen of Summer feel sad, and she allowed herself to be seen. "Glooscap," she said, "we cannot let the Ice King melt to death. Is there a way he can be allowed to live without harming the Wabanaki?"

"There is a way if all agree," said Glooscap. "The Ice King must go farther north for six months of the year while you warm this part of the world. At the end of six months, the Ice King can return. This will be a good thing for it will give my people a time to work and a time to have pleasure. This way they will not become lazy."

"This will be good for my people too," agreed the Queen of Summer.

And so it was decided. The Ice King made a new home farther north, while the Queen of Summer followed the moose hide back to the South Land. Glooscap returned to his people, who were now thankful to have the gift of different seasons.

## SEASONS

The Earth is really moving! It travels in an almost circular orbit around the Sun once each year and rotates on its axis, each turn equaling one day. The axis is always at a 23.5-degree tilt (picture a spinning top, with one side forever tipped in the same direction). This tilt is what causes the seasons. When the tilt faces the Sun, the Sun is higher in the sky and its sunlight strikes the Earth more directly. This creates longer days, and summer occurs. When the Earth's tilt faces away from the Sun, the Sun is lower in the sky. As a result, the days are shorter and we experience winter.

Each season lasts about three months. The seasons occur at opposite times to each other in each hemisphere (the northern and southern halves of the Earth). When the North Pole is tilted toward the Sun, summer occurs in the Northern Hemisphere because the Sun's rays strike that part of the Earth more directly. The South Pole is pointed away from the Sun at this time, so the Southern Hemisphere does not receive as much direct sunlight.

The lengths of day and night also influence temperature. Long summer days mean the Sun has more time to warm an area, while short winter days are followed by long, cold winter nights.

CONTINUED . . .

The Earth is divided into imaginary lines called degrees of longitude, which run east and west, and degrees of latitude, which run north and south. The distance between the lines, called parallels, are measured in degrees, minutes, and seconds. The equator, which divides the Earth into the Northern and Southern Hemispheres, is at zero degrees. All other points are described as north or south of the equator. Some lines are given names, such as the Arctic and Antarctic Circles, the Tropic of Cancer (23.5 degrees north of the equator), and the Tropic of Capricorn (23.5 degrees south of the equator). The Sun's travel is described according to its location over the Earth. At the equator, the Sun is directly overhead at noon.

The solstices mark the longest and shortest days of the year. In the Northern Hemisphere, the summer solstice is the first day of summer. It occurs when the Sun crosses the sky above the Tropic of Cancer, around June 21. The winter solstice is the first day of winter and takes place around December 21, when the Sun crosses the sky above the Tropic of Capricorn. When the summer solstice occurs in the Northern Hemisphere, there are 24 hours of sunlight in the northernmost parts of the globe, and 24 hours of darkness in the southernmost parts. The opposite occurs when the Northern Hemisphere experiences the winter solstice.

The equinox marks the two times each year when day and night are of equal length—each 12 hours long. The autumn equinox occurs around September 23 and marks the first day of fall in the Northern Hemisphere and the first day of spring in the Southern Hemisphere. The vernal equinox occurs around March 21 and marks the first day of spring in the Northern Hemisphere and the first day of fall in the Southern Hemisphere.

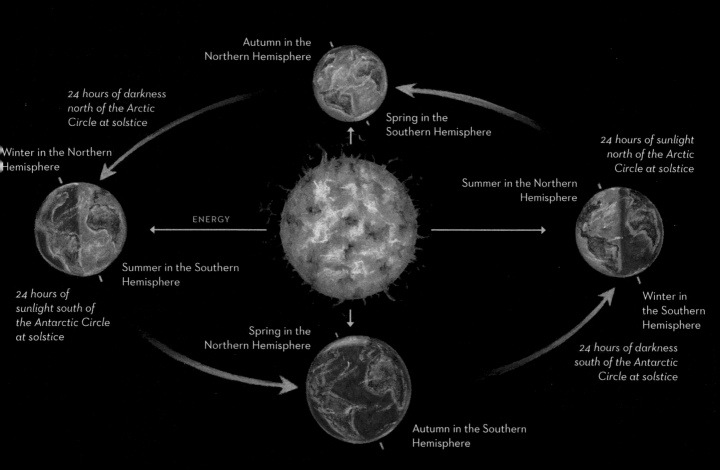

Autumn in the
Northern Hemisphere

*24 hours of darkness
north of the Arctic
Circle at solstice*

Spring in the
Southern Hemisphere

*24 hours of sunlight
north of the Arctic
Circle at solstice*

Winter in the Northern
Hemisphere

Summer in the Northern
Hemisphere

ENERGY

Summer in the Southern
Hemisphere

Winter in
the Southern
Hemisphere

*24 hours of
sunlight south of
the Antarctic Circle
at solstice*

Spring in the
Northern Hemisphere

*24 hours of darkness
south of the Antarctic
Circle at solstice*

Autumn in the Southern
Hemisphere

Both hemispheres tend to have moderate weather in the spring and fall because all parts of the Earth receive roughly the same number of hours of sunlight and darkness.

Only the areas located north and south of the tropics experience four seasons. Between the Tropic of Cancer and the Tropic of Capricorn, the two seasons are defined as the rainy season or the dry season. It stays warm and humid throughout the year because, for these areas, the Sun is never very low in the sky.

Axis
North Pole

Arctic Cirle

Tropic of Cancer

Equator

Tropic of Capricorn

Antarctic Circle

South Pole

# Father Frost

—— ☁ ——

## {RUSSIAN}

ONCE UPON A time in a cold and far away part of Russia, a young maiden named Martha lived with her father and his second wife. The stepmother had two daughters of her own and treated them with great care, but took no time to show love to anyone else. Her daughters were rather ugly but she dressed them in pretty frocks and gave them sweets to make them smile. Martha, meanwhile, was left to wear their outgrown rags and eat their leftovers.

The stepsisters learned how to be unkind from their mother. They did not feel at all guilty if they forgot to share, or if the dog ate their scraps before their stepsister had eaten. The stepsisters ordered Martha to fetch things for them and made fun of her whenever they saw the chance. Life was not very pleasant for the poor girl, but she tried to be cheerful and not let them break her spirit.

Unfortunately, Martha's father did not have a strong will. He wanted a quiet home, and tried to avoid arguing with his wife at all times, even though his daughter was treated poorly. One cold winter day, when the wind blew snow from every direction, the stepmother decided Martha could not live with them anymore. Her daughters were getting to the age where young men would be coming to call, and the stepmother did not want the more-beautiful Martha to be in the way.

Martha's stepmother ordered her husband to ready the horses and sleigh and come to the front of the house. Without asking why, he did as she asked. Opening the front door, he announced, "The sleigh is ready. What errand are you sending me to do?"

The stepmother pushed Martha out the door and replied, "Take your daughter deep into the forest. Go as far as the trail will take you, then walk her into the trees until you can walk no more. Leave her there and return. Her betrothed will find her." The husband knew his daughter could never survive in the storm but he was so afraid of his wife's anger that he helped his daughter into the sleigh and drove deep into the forest.

Martha and her father traveled as far as the trail would take them, then pushed through the snow until they could walk no more. After resting for a short time, the father kissed his daughter on the forehead and sorrowfully walked back to the sleigh to return home.

Alone in a clearing where the snowdrifts rose like frozen waves, the maiden sat upon a stump. The wind blew and ice crackled as it fell from the trees. The chilling cold seeped through her thin clothes.

Suddenly, the wind whirled around her and a voice asked, "Are you warm, young maiden in the snowy mist?" Realizing it could only be Father Frost, the maiden politely answered, "I am very comfortable, thank you." Father Frost made icy flakes sweep across the clearing in a chilling gust of wind and asked again, "Are you warm, young maiden in the snowy mist?"

"Indeed, I am very comfortable, thank you," she replied.

Winter clouds suddenly blew across the sky and sharp crystal flakes hailed down upon Martha. Father Frost came closer, his icy breath frosting the maiden's hair as he asked, "Are you truly warm, young maiden in the snowy mist?"

"Truly, I am very comfortable, thank you Father Frost," replied Martha.

Father Frost looked closely at the maiden who would not complain and appreciated her politeness. He used his winter magic to envelop her in a blanket so thick that she became as warm as she needed to be. The stump upon which she had leaned became a magnificent chair embroidered with gold thread, and a chest of precious jewels and gifts appeared at her feet. Father Frost disappeared up into his storm clouds and drifted further north.

The next day, the maiden's father returned to look for his daughter. He was so happy to find Martha safe and alive, he clasped her close and spun about in a circle. Laughing with joy, he lifted her into the sleigh and piled the gifts behind them.

When they got home and Martha's stepmother saw that she was not only alive but also wealthy, she insisted her husband take her own daughters into the forest that night. When the Sun went down, he helped his stepdaughters into the sleigh and drove them deep into the forest. They traveled as far as the trail would take them, then pushed through the snow until they could walk no further. Left in the very same clearing as their stepsister, the daughters waited for good fortune to appear.

The Sun set and the wind picked up. Alone in the clearing where the snowdrifts rose like frozen waves, the daughters sat upon two stumps. The wind blew and ice crackled as it fell from the trees. The chilling cold seeped through their thick coats and stiffened their toes inside their heavy winter boots. Suddenly the wind whirled around them. A voice came close and asked, "Are you warm, young maidens in the snowy mist?" The first daughter replied straightaway: "Certainly not. It is fearsomely cold and I wish the wind would stop."

Father Frost was not pleased. He made icy flakes sweep across the clearing in a chilling gust of wind and asked again, "Are you warm, young maidens in the snowy mist?"

"Not one bit!" replied the second daughter. "Winter is the most miserable season. I cannot wait for it to end."

Father Frost curled his lips in a grimace. Winter clouds suddenly blew across the sky and sharp, crystal flakes, hailed down upon the maidens. Father Frost came closer, his icy breath frosting each maiden's head as he asked, "Is there nothing you like about winter, young maidens in the snowy mist?"

"There is not one thing to like about winter," the maidens chorused. Enraged, Father Frost blew a storm so powerful that the wind twirled the snowy flakes into hard-packed drifts as high as the trees.

The next day, the girls' stepfather took the sleigh into the forest to bring them back. Making his way over and around the drifts, he trudged to the clearing in the forest, and found their frozen bodies in the snow. He put them in the sleigh and returned home.

The maidens' mother ran up to the sleigh, anxious to see what riches her daughters now owned. When she saw the frozen bodies she flew into a terrible rage. Blaming her husband, she began to shout cruel insults at him. Finally he spoke his mind.

"Martha is a kind girl with kind words for all she meets, even Father Frost. Now she has been rewarded, while your daughters, who never had a good word to say about anything, have been punished. It is certainly too late for them. Is it too late for you?"

The stepmother became quiet. No one had ever spoken to her this way before. She thought about his words for a long time and changed her ways as much as she could.

Martha married and had children, always reminding them to practice the habit of using kind words. She told them, "You never know what power a stranger might wield."

## FROST LORE

- In Russian folklore, Father Frost is a blacksmith who bound the Earth and sea with great chains of ice.

- Jokul Frosti, which means icicle frost, was the son of the Nordic wind god Kari. Also called Jack Frost, he was known for leaving lacy white patterns on windows.

- In German folklore, Old Mother Frost made snow by shaking out her white feather bed.

- An Australian Aborigine story tells of the seven sisters who form the Pleiades star cluster. They take icicles from their sparkling bodies and hurl them down to Earth.

# FROST

 Frost is the covering of tiny ice crystals on a cold surface like grass, trees, or cars. It usually occurs after a clear night when there are no clouds to trap warm air near the Earth's surface, and it only forms when the temperature is below freezing (32°F/0°C). Thick, white hoar frost sometimes resembles snow. It forms after sunset when a temperature drop causes moist air near the ground to cool to below freezing and immediately form ice crystals.

 Water in plants freezes during a frost. A killing frost is one that is strong enough to kill plants or end the growing season. When a killing frost is predicted, gardeners often protect their plants by covering them overnight with old sheets or blankets. Orchard owners may save their fruit by burning oil or using fans to help move warm air around the trees. Large fruit-growing operations might arrange to have a helicopter fly over the orchard at night. The helicopter's propellers keep air moving, while heat from the exhaust adds a bit of warmth.

# How the Fog Came

{INUIT}

LONG AGO, IN the far north where the Inuit people live, a mountain spirit was said to haunt a graveyard. The spirit was said to watch and wait until a burial took place, then later that night float across the graveyard right up to the fresh grave. It would dig into the ground, lift the body from its resting place, and drag it back to its home on the mountain.

The Inuit people were not very happy when they found overturned earth beside empty graves. They wondered why a spirit would steal the bodies of their families and friends. No one could understand why a spirit would do such a thing.

One man did not believe the stories about the mountain spirit. He wondered if perhaps a wild beast or even a person was stealing the bodies from the graves. After it happened three times in one month, he decided to see what he could find out about the thief.

The man went to the graveyard, dug a hole as long as his body, and lay down inside the hollow. He carefully reached his arms out of the hole and brushed dirt over himself, leaving a small airway so he could breathe.

The man waited. The Sun set and the air became cool. The ground felt damp as it pushed against him. Bits of soil tickled his neck and the smell of the freshly turned earth filled his nostrils. His legs were getting stiff but he did not think of getting up. Despite the discomfort, he was determined to find out if the mysterious spirit was really a ghost or in fact some sort of beast.

Finally, just as the man began to think he could not endure the discomfort any longer, the earth over top of him began to move. He closed his eyes so it would appear as though he were truly dead, and after a moment the cold night air blew against his skin. The man felt himself lifted into the air and thrown across a furry back. Slowly opening his eyes into narrow slits, he saw he was held by a massive bear nearly twice his height.

The bear carried the man towards some woods and entered a path leading through a willow thicket. Branches stuck into the path, but the bear pushed through them. His fur was too thick for him to feel their jabs. Each time the man was able to reach one of the willow branches sticking into the path, he grabbed hold and held it just long enough to make the bear stagger from his weight. Each time this happened, the bear would have to heave him up again. He hoped to tire the bear out, thinking if he found a way to escape the bear might be too tired to chase after him.

At last the bear reached his home where he lived with his mate and two cubs—a shelter beneath some logs that had fallen over a bank. The bear threw the man on the mossy ground inside the den, planning to eat him later. For the moment he only wanted to sleep.

Muscles sore and stiff from being carried, the man did not mind lying still. Suddenly he felt a wet nose push into his arm. The female bear was sniffing him. It tickled so much, he almost laughed out loud, but stopped himself by imagining what would happen if he got caught.

Sniffing the man until she was satisfied he would make a tasty meal, the bear lumbered outside to gather some firewood for cooking. The two cubs watched until she was out of sight. The man heard her steps upon the leaves outside the den. Not knowing two cubs were watching, he opened his eyes and began to sit up.

"Papa! The man is alive! Look! Look!" they chorused.

The man immediately slumped to the floor and pretended to be dead again.

The cub's father did not like being disturbed when he slept. "He is certainly not alive," said the bear. "I dug him from a grave and carried his dead weight all the way here. Go help your mother, go play in the woods, but whatever you choose, do not disturb me when I'm sleeping!"

The cubs were afraid of their father's temper. They ran outside and the bear growled himself back to sleep. As soon as he was silent and breathing steadily, the man stood up. He carefully lifted a sturdy log from the ground and struck the bear hard on the head. That was the end of the grave-stealing bear. The man ran from the den just as the she-bear returned, her arms laden with branches.

Bears do not have very good eyesight and she thought her husband was the one racing from the yard. "Where are you running to? How long will you be gone?" she called.

The man did not answer, so she dropped the firewood and chased after him.

The man glanced over his shoulder and saw the bear getting close. He shouted to the ground for help, "Rise up, ground!" Immediately hills formed behind him and the bear started to lag as she climbed hill after hill. But the bear had four legs and the man only had two, so after some time she began to catch up to him.

Glancing back, the man saw she was getting close again. He jumped across a small creek, then turned back. "Flow across the land," he shouted at the creek. The water immediately began to overflow the creek bed. It churned and bubbled downstream so swiftly that the bear could not get to the other bank.

"How did you get across?" the bear called, still thinking she was chasing her mate.

"I drank from the creek," shouted the man. "You must drink until there is no water left."

The bear lowered her head to the water. She drank and drank until her body began to swell and her belly began to slosh. She felt quite full, but the creek continued to flow. She stopped to catch her breath. The man looked back and saw her resting.

"Now jump high into the air!" he shouted.

The bear jumped as high as she could but her body was too full of water. She fell back to the ground with a great big splat. Water exploded out of the bear's body and formed a fog so thick she could not see the man, the creek, or even her own paws. The man escaped into the fog and returned home,

while the bear used her sense of smell to find her way back to her cubs. They returned to the den and realized they had been tricked by the man who was not dead.

From that day on, graves were never disturbed and the Inuit were thankful for the man who had shown the courage to seek the truth. And to this day, fog still floats above the ground and never fully disappears. People who remember the grave-robbing spirit do not mind, for they would rather have fog around them than a thief.

## FOG

- Fog is a cloud on the ground that is usually created when air at the Earth's surface is a lot colder than the air higher up. Driving and landing aircraft can be dangerous because it is difficult to see through fog.

- Fog is called a mist when it's thin enough for you to see about 0.5 to 6 miles (1 to 10 kilometers) into the distance.

- A fog will begin to evaporate when the Sun heats the ground near the fog's edge. Some sunlight gets through the fog and warms the ground, causing the part of the fog nearest the ground to disappear first.

- Fog, smoke, and pollutants in the air combine to produce a type of air pollution called smog.

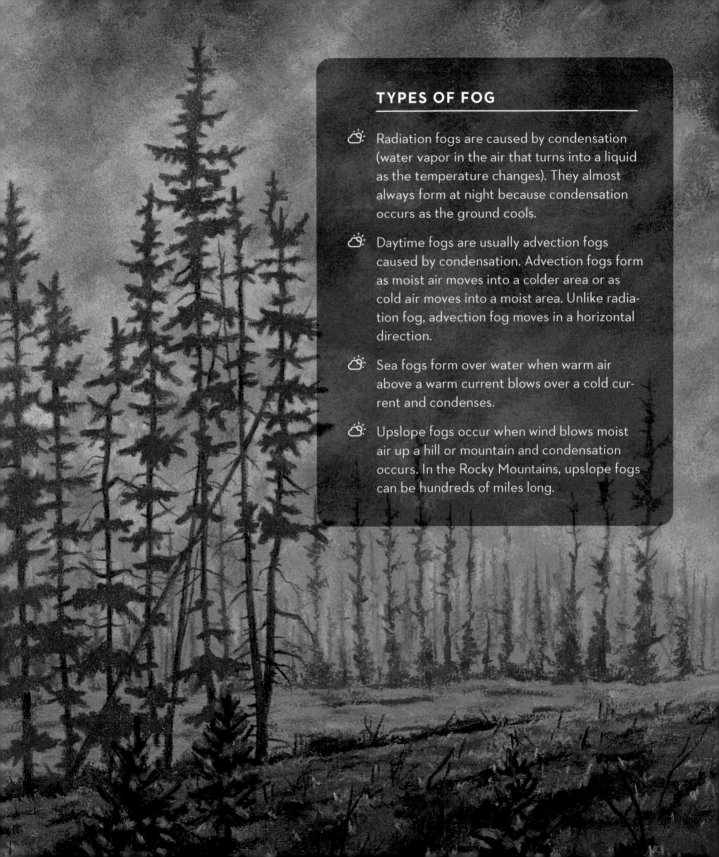

## TYPES OF FOG

- Radiation fogs are caused by condensation (water vapor in the air that turns into a liquid as the temperature changes). They almost always form at night because condensation occurs as the ground cools.

- Daytime fogs are usually advection fogs caused by condensation. Advection fogs form as moist air moves into a colder area or as cold air moves into a moist area. Unlike radiation fog, advection fog moves in a horizontal direction.

- Sea fogs form over water when warm air above a warm current blows over a cold current and condenses.

- Upslope fogs occur when wind blows moist air up a hill or mountain and condensation occurs. In the Rocky Mountains, upslope fogs can be hundreds of miles long.

# Embrace the Weather

─────── ☁ ───────

**WHETHER THE AIR** is scorching, frosty, clear, foggy, overcast, or stormy, there's always something interesting happening in the Earth's atmosphere. Take the time to observe the sky. If it is safe, go outdoors to experience the weather every day. Observe the clouds, watch how they move across the sky, and see how many types of cloud you can spot. Feel the wind and determine what direction it comes from most often. Close your eyes and listen. How does rain sound different on grass, pavement, or other surfaces? Can you hear snow as it falls or melts? How many weather sounds can you list? Sniff the air and notice how different temperatures and conditions smell, and how they make your skin feel. Can you sense a change in the air during certain kinds of weather?

Now, imagine what it would be like if you lived long ago, during a time when survival was even more closely tied to the weather, and your senses and beliefs were essential to understanding the conditions around you. Without science, you might have created stories to understand the Sun, wind, and storms too!

The weather will always be an important part of our lives, and scientists will continue to discover awe-inspiring facts about how our natural world works. When you step outside and examine the sky, think of those scientific facts alongside the stories ancient cultures once told, and embrace every type of weather.

## DISCOVER MORE ONLINE

THE AUTHOR'S WEBSITE www.joangalat.com

CLIMATE KIDS – NASA'S EYES ON THE EARTH https://climatekids.nasa.gov

SCIJINKS https://scijinks.gov

WEB WEATHER FOR KIDS https://eo.ucar.edu/webweather

# Glossary

— ☁ —

**AIR MASS** a body of air with nearly the same temperature and humidity throughout. Air masses can be as high as the stratosphere and hundreds or thousands of miles long.

**AIR PRESSURE** the force caused by air particles as they bounce against each other and their surroundings. Barometers measure this force in pascals or pounds per square inch.

**ATMOSPHERE** the air held close to the Earth by gravity.

**AXIS** an imaginary line around which a body such as the Earth rotates.

**CIRRUS** white, wispy clouds usually containing very small ice crystals and found 20,000 to 40,000 feet (6,000 to 12,000 meters) above the Earth.

**CLIMATE** a location's average type of weather over a period of years.

**CLOUD** a cluster of water and/or ice particles that can be seen suspended in the atmosphere.

**CONDENSE** to change from a gas to a liquid.

**CONDENSATION** the process that occurs when a temperature change causes water vapor to turn to liquid.

**CONDUCTOR** an object that an electric current can flow through.

**CONVECTION** movement of a gas or liquid where the warmer portions rise and the cooler portions sink.

**CUMULUS** a dense, fluffy looking cloud with a flat base and rounded outlines.

**CYCLONE** a windstorm that rotates counterclockwise in the Northern Hemisphere and clockwise in the Southern Hemisphere.

**EQUATOR** an imaginary circle around the center of the Earth that divides the Northern and Southern Hemispheres.

**EQUINOX** the two days each year when the day and night are of equal length (12 hours each). The autumnal equinox occurs around September 23 and the vernal equinox occurs around March 21.

**FOG** a cloud on the ground, usually created when air at the Earth's surface is much colder than air higher up.

**FROST** tiny ice crystals that form on a surface that is below freezing and colder than the surrounding air.

**HEMISPHERE** the northern or southern half of the Earth.

**HIGH-PRESSURE AREA** a region where dry, cool air creates fair weather and light winds.

**HUMIDITY** the amount of moisture in the air.

**HURRICANE** a huge storm or system of winds that rotates and travels 75 miles (120 kilometers) per hour or greater, often with heavy rain, thunder, and lightning. Hurricanes are tropical cyclones that form over the Atlantic Ocean or eastern Pacific Ocean, span several thousand miles, and last several days.

**LATITUDE** the distance north or south of the Earth's equator.

**LIGHTNING** a flash of light caused by an electric current in the atmosphere.

**LOW-PRESSURE AREA** a region where moist, warm air creates stormy weather and strong winds.

**METEOROLOGIST** a scientist who studies the atmosphere, weather patterns, and ways to predict what weather will occur.

**METEOROLOGY** the science that deals with the atmosphere and weather conditions.

**NORTH POLE** the Earth's northernmost point.

**OZONE LAYER** a layer of ozone in the stratosphere that stops harmful radiation from the Sun from reaching Earth's surface.

**PRECIPITATION** moisture that falls as rain, snow, ice pellets, or hail depending on air temperature and currents. Precipitation occurs when water droplets become too heavy for the air to hold up any longer.

**SEASON** a period of time defined by a certain type of weather.

**SMOG** a type of air pollution produced when fog, smoke, and pollutants combine in the air.

**SNOW** precipitation made up of hexagon-shaped ice crystals formed from frozen water vapor.

**SOLSTICE** when the Sun is at its most distant point from the celestial equator, occurring on the longest and shortest days of the year. In the Northern Hemisphere, the summer solstice occurs around June 21, the first day of summer, and the winter solstice takes place around December 21, the first day of winter.

**SOUTH POLE** the Earth's southernmost point.

**STRATOSPHERE** the part of the Earth's atmosphere stretching from the top of the troposphere to about 30 miles (50 kilometers) above the Earth's surface.

**STRATUS** a low cloud that extends over a large area, usually at heights from 2,000 to 7,000 feet (600 to 2,100 meters) above the Earth's surface.

**TEMPERATURE** a degree of hotness or coldness measured using the Fahrenheit or Celsius scale.

**THUNDER** the sound associated with a flash of lightning, caused when air suddenly expands and contracts.

**THUNDERSTORM** a storm that produces thunder and lightning with potential for heavy rain, high winds, hail, or tornadoes.

**TORNADO** a violent and destructive whirling wind, seen as a funnel-shaped cloud crossing over land in a path tens to hundreds of yards (meters) wide.

**TROPIC OF CANCER** the northernmost latitude at which the Sun can pass directly overhead, approximately 23.5 degrees north of the equator.

**TROPIC OF CAPRICORN** the southernmost latitude at which the Sun can pass directly overhead, approximately 23.5 degrees south of the equator.

**TROPOSPHERE** the densest part of the Earth's atmosphere, where most weather changes occur. The troposphere reaches from the Earth's surface to 11 miles (17 kilometers) above sea level over the equator and about 5 miles (8 kilometers) above sea level over the poles.

**TYPHOON** a tropical cyclone occurring around the Philippines or the China Sea.

**WATER VAPOR** water in the form of gas.

**WEATHER** the state of the atmosphere with respect to heat or cold, wetness or dryness, calmness or storminess, clearness or cloudiness.

**WIND** the movement of air caused by differences in air pressure.

# Acknowledgments

─────── ☁ ───────

THANK YOU TO the Alberta Foundation for the Arts for its much appreciated financial support during the research and writing of *Stories in the Clouds;* Patrick Geraghty, Whitecap Books editor, whose literary expertise enriched both science and stories; Georgia Graham for her compelling and irresistable artwork; and the meterology experts who generously gave their time to answer my questions.

J.M.G.

# Index

— ☁ —

## ABOUT THE AUTHOR

CREDIT Rob Hislop Photography.

JOAN MARIE GALAT lives in the Alberta countryside near Edmonton, where she can often be found gazing upwards. She shares her love of the sky in the *Dot to Dot in the Sky* series, which offers both science and stories from ancient cultures about our environment and the night sky.

Joan's writing career began with a weekly newspaper column when she was 12 years old. Now an award-winning and best-selling author, she has written more than a dozen books for both children and adults. She provides freelance writing and editing through her communications business, MoonDot Media, and is a frequent presenter at schools and libraries.

While Alberta's long winter nights and big prairie sky are ideal for stargazing, Joan also enjoys other pastimes such as reading, camping, kayaking, spending time outdoors, and even stiltwalking. She likes to travel and picnic, which led to her book *Day Trips from Edmonton*.

Visit Joan's websites at www.joangalat.com and www.moondot-media.com for details on her books, presentations, and writing workshops.

## ABOUT THE ILLUSTRATOR

CREDIT Marlene Palamarek Photography 2017.

GEORGIA GRAHAM has been a compulsive drawer ever since she was a child growing up in Calgary, Alberta. She graduated from the Alberta College of Art in 1982 where she majored in Visual Communications. She has written and illustrated *Cub's Journey Home, Where Wild Horses Run, The Lime Green Secret, A Team Like No Other,* and *The Strongest Man This Side of Cremona,* as well as illustrating many children's books by other authors. Her books often reflect Alberta's landscape, communities, farms, and ranches. She illustrates in chalk pastel on sanded paper and paints with acrylic on canvas. Her books and art can be viewed at www.georgiagraham.com.

Georgia lives with her husband on a small farm on the edge of Lacombe, Alberta. Her grown children and granddaughter live nearby.